FIFTY OVER 50

Inspirational profiles of people passionately
pursuing new purpose later in life

*Compiled from public sources or personal interviews
by the staff at Forward From 50.*

GREG GERBER

Copyright © 2022 by Forward From 50, LLC

Forward From 50
PO Box 2002
Sun City, AZ 85372
www.forwardfrom50.com
info@forwardfrom50.com

ISBN: 978-1-7344738-2-7 (Softcover)
ISBN: 978-1-7344738-3-4 (Ebook)

Publisher:
Faithfire Media

"It's not enough to have lived.
We should be determined to live for something."

– Winston S. Churchill

INTRODUCTION

There is something about our culture today that wants to nudge people out the door or to the sidelines once they reach the half-century mark. But, that's such a waste of wisdom and experience they've accumulated throughout their lives.

Many times, we abandoned things in our youth that really fired us up and gave us a sense of purpose just to embrace more practical jobs out of a sense of duty or necessity when raising a family. Often, that passion still burns within us — even if it's just a smoldering wick.

Turning 50 is the ideal time to rekindle that fire!

As "seasoned citizens," we've done our jobs in raising children, and we've played the corporate game of hustling and striving for little reward or appreciation. Let's face it, we are tired of running on the hamster wheel of life.

We want our lives to count for something and to know with certainty that our brief time on earth really mattered. We know in our hearts that we still have lots of life left to live. In our spirits, we are still as young today as the day we left the security of home to take on a big, bold world.

Unfortunately, when we step off that hamster wheel, we are often unprepared for the next chapter in our lives. Golfing and fishing all day may sound relaxing, and so is meeting friends for lunch. But the lack of meaningful activity often leaves us wondering, "Is there more to life than this?"

The answer is a resounding YES!

This booklet outlines brief profiles of fifty men and women who discovered a renewed sense of purpose after their 50th birthdays. Some of the folks mentioned are well into their 70s, 80s and beyond.

You were created for a specific purpose and instilled with unique traits to help you accomplish that purpose. The challenges that forged your character, the experiences that pushed you to embrace new opportunities, the people who came into and out of your life — everything you've endured so far — has prepared you for this moment.

So, if you're at a stage in life where you wonder if you still have anything meaningful to contribute to the world, rest assured each of these men and women felt the same way. Then, one day, an opportunity presented itself that seemed ideally suited for their unique skills talent and life experiences.

Stepping out on faith to pursue that idea or smoldering desire made all the difference in their lives and to the lives of others. These go-getters found success or fulfillment by following their dreams even when the world was encouraging them to slow down and take it easy.

May their stories inspire you to step out of your comfort zone to embrace the greatness hidden within you. Remember, you were designed for more!

GREG GERBER
Founder, Forward From 50

"The two most important days in life are the day you were born and the day you discover the reason why."

– Mark Twain

RICHARD ADAMS

A MADE UP STORY FOR HIS GIRLS BECOMES A BEST-SELLING BOOK

Born in 1920 near Berkshire, England, Richard Adams lived a relatively obscure life working for the British army and as a housing official. He also served as an environmental agent, which became a source of inspiration for his future writing.

As a hobby, Richard would write stories in his spare time, which he would then read to his daughters, Juliet and Rosamond. One of their favorites was about a group of bunnies who formed their own language, culture, community, leadership and life lessons which the rabbits passed down from generation to generation.

He later admitted the stories were created off the top of his head, but they mesmerized his daughters on long car trips. The girls insisted that he write the impromptu stories down so they could be shared with other children.

Photo by Gary Bendig at Unsplash

Richard was 48 when he finished the manuscript for *Watership Down*. But it was rejected by four publishers and three writers' agencies before finally being published in 1972 when Richard was 52 years old.

According to Wikipedia, the book explores themes like exile, survival, community, leadership, political responsibility and the making of a hero. His writing was highly praised for its ability to assign human qualities to animals, and for the rabbits' spell-binding adventures as well as their relationships.

Watership Down sold more than a million copies and Richard earned the Carnegie Medal and Guardian Children's Fiction Prize, becoming one of six authors to receive both prestigious awards.

The book's success allowed Richard to leave his civil service job to become a full-time writer. *Watership Down* was turned into a motion picture and animated television series. He published more than 20 books before his death in 2016 at the age of 96.

MOMOFUKU ANDO

HIS POST-WAR INVENTION BECOMES A HOUSEHOLD STAPLE

Born into a wealthy Taiwanese family in 1910, Momofuku Ando was raised by his grandparents after the death of his parents. They owned a small textile store, which inspired him to pursue starting his own store at the age of 22.

He later traveled to Japan to study economics while launching a clothing company. Momofuku lost that company in 1948 after being charged for tax evasion and serving two years in jail because he provided scholarships for students, which was against the law at the time.

Upon his release, Momofuku started over by founding Nissin, a small family-run company that produced salt products.

When Japan experienced a shortage of food after World War II, the government encouraged people to eat bread made from wheat supplied by the United States, Wikipedia noted. However, Momofuku wondered why officials weren't recommending noodles, which were more familiar to Japanese people. They told him companies manufacturing noodles were too small and unstable to meet the high demand. So, he developed a way to produce noodles himself.

Photo from Adobe Stock

At the age of 48, after months of experimentation, he perfected a flash-frying method and marketed the first instant noodles under the Chikin Ramen brand. However, the product was expensive and sold for nearly six times the price of traditional noodles.

He kept refining his process before inventing Cup Noodles in 1971 when he was 61 years old. They were instantly popular, especially in America. According to Wikipedia, Momofuku observed that Americans ate noodles by breaking them in half, putting them into a paper cup, adding hot water and eating them with a fork instead of chopsticks.

He was inspired to use a Styrofoam cup to hold the noodles, which also worked to keep them warmer and make it easier to hold a hot cup. People would consume the product by opening the lid, adding hot water and waiting. By 2009, worldwide demand for Cup Noodles exceeded 98 billion servings annually.

Momofuku also founded the Instant Food Industry Association, which set guidelines for fair competition and product quality as well as establishing several industry standards, like inclusion of production dates on packaging and a "fill to" line.

DAVE AND TRUDY BATEMAN

A HEAVENLY FONDNESS FOR COFFEE AND A SIMPLE LIFE

For more than 35 years, Dave Bateman spent much of his career as a lawyer. He served in the U.S. Air Force where he rose to the rank of colonel and worked as a Washington State assistant attorney general for a while. However, it was a private client who changed Dave's life by inviting him to visit a coffee farm on Kona, Hawaii. The client needed legal advice for his new venture.

Feeling the effects of corporate burnout, Dave found the farm to be a peaceful respite. When he sipped coffee grown on the farm, he was sold on the business as a wonderful opportunity – for himself and his wife, Trudy. They purchased the 38-acre Heavenly Hawaiian Farm in 2005 when they were both in their late 50s.

Growing coffee is vastly different from litigating legal cases and working as an emergency room nurse, which is what Trudy did for a living. So they spent the first year of self-employment learning the ropes from its previous owner. The couple learned how to drive and repair tractors as well as manage every aspect of farm operation from fertilizing soil to effectively pruning more than 24,000 coffee trees.

Photo by Pariwat Pannium on Unsplash

In 2021, the farm employed six full-time workers and more than a dozen seasonal pickers to produce 250,000 pounds of green and roasted coffee annually, which is then sold around the world.

One of Dave's favorite sayings is, "A bad day on the coffee farm is a whole lot better than a good day in the courtroom."

HARRY BERNSTEIN

A PUBLISHED AUTHOR AT 96

Born in England in 1910, Harry Bernstein later moved to America where he worked as a script reader for several movie production companies. He also wrote stories for magazines like *Family Circle*, *Newsweek* and *Popular Mechanics*.

But, he didn't make his true mark on the world until Harry published his first book at the age of 96.

The Invisible Wall paid tribute to his mother's struggle to feed six children despite being trapped in an abusive relationship with his alcoholic father. It also described the anti-Semitism his Jewish family experienced in northwest England, especially as it pertained to the relationship his sister had with her Christian boyfriend.

Harry started writing the book when he was 93 following the death of his wife, Ruby, in 2002. It was a way to combat loneliness without the woman who was a major part of his life for more than 67 years.

Photo by Sonder Quest on Unsplash

He went on to publish two other books. *The Dream* was a memoir focused on his family's miraculous move to the west side of Chicago when he was 12 years old, thanks to free steamship tickets from an anonymous benefactor. The family's pursuit of the American Dream was detoured by the Great Depression, which forced them to move to New York where they eventually enjoyed success.

The Golden Willow was Harry's memoir about his own love story about meeting Ruby and their rollercoaster life that united them even stronger. He died while working on a fourth book at the age of 101.

"When you get into your 90s, like I am, there's nowhere else to think except the past. There's no future to think about. There's very little present," Harry told *South Coast Today*. "So you think of the past, particularly at nighttime when you're lying in bed. And it all came back. So I began to write, and I was occupied. It was really the best therapy I could have had."

JANET BLACK

TURNING PAIN INTO PURPOSE

Before turning 50, it took Janet Black quite some time to figure out what she wanted to be when she grew up. Ultimately, she combined her love for science with her desire to help others and become a nurse practitioner.

Unfortunately, she developed fibromyalgia, a medical condition which causes increased pain throughout her body and can also result in cognitive issues as well as sleep problems.

"I was having problems with what is called 'fibro fog' to the point I couldn't remember things," Janet told Forward From 50. "I was concerned I could make a mistake that would wind up hurting a patient, so I decided to quit."

After stepping away from nursing, Janet sat around feeling depressed for several years. When she was approved for Social Security disability payments on her first try, it caused even more depression by making her realize the severity of her condition.

Then Janet turned her sights on writing. She had been mulling a number of book ideas for years. In fact, she wrote one several years earlier to help teens and tweens who were victims of sexual abuse.

"There really wasn't anything out there in the way of books to help teenagers recover from sexual abuse. There was a lot of material for adults and a

Photo provided by Janet Black

few resources for young children, but nothing for teens. So, I wrote one," she explained.

Because she couldn't find a traditional publisher at the time, Janet tucked the manuscript away. Now that her career was over, she pulled it out of the file, polished it up and decided to self-publish the book. Since then, she has written books about fibromyalgia, weight loss, living in a toxic world and homelessness, which was a book she co-authored with her husband.

For Janet, it feels really good to have created something from nothing, especially when the book helps someone else.

"I have to do something with my creative energy because I can't just sit around all day and do nothing," she explained. "I volunteered for different projects in the past, but it just feels even better to know that something I wrote is actually helping educate people about a topic I'm interested in writing about."

WALLY BLUME

FOUNDER OF MOOSE TRACKS ICE CREAM

After 23 years in the grocery business, where part of his responsibilities involved overseeing dairy products for Kroger, Wally Blume accepted a new job selling ingredients to create various ice cream flavors and package them in special containers.

A few years later in 1988, at the age of 54, Wally developed a novel ice cream flavor which proved to be widely popular. It blended vanilla ice cream with peanut butter cups and bits of salty dark chocolate fudge. He called it Moose Tracks, in tribute to an Upper Michigan miniature golf course near the first dairy to serve his frozen concoction.

Within eight years, the Moose Tracks flavor was being produced by 34 regional dairy plants, and Wally formed Denali Flavors with two business partners to create even more unique ice cream ingredients. At the age of 62, he bought out his two partners so he could grow the business with his wife, June.

Photo from Adobe Stock

Together, they added additional flavors, including a Moose Tracks version made with chocolate ice cream. In total, they created more than 30 different flavored dessert treats which were manufactured at 84 regional dairy plants nationwide.

In 2006, the company bought out a former Eskimo Pie manufacturing facility in Berlin, Wis., and changed its name to Denali Ingredients to supply raw materials to bakeries and other food service production facilities.

At 76, Wally was still heavily involved with the business in 2021 and looking to expand even further by partnering with a nut company to offer a new line of ready-to-eat snacks for sale in grocery and convenience stores.

Crediting their Christian faith, which motivated Wally to launch their business in the first place, he and June share their faith daily one scoop at a time.

"The goal for our business is to fund the gospel and to bring people into the kingdom," he told the *700 Club*.

LYNN BROOKS

MAKING VISITORS COMFORTABLE IN THE BIG APPLE

A native of New York City, Lynn Brooks loved The Big Apple and she wanted others to fall in love with its charm as well. However, she knew many people were apprehensive about spending time in America's largest city. It had a horrible reputation, and she sought to change that perception one person at a time.

She wanted people to understand New York the way she did by discovering the beautiful life hidden in the big city. So, in 1992, at the age of 56, she founded Big Apple Greeters to help improve New York City's reputation with outsiders and visitors.

At first, Lynn and her family volunteered to greet tourists and offer helpful advice about places to visit. Other New York fans quickly stepped in to help, too. They'd spend several hours with single visitors, families and small groups recommending their favorite restaurants, stores or attractions and offering tips on how to best navigate the city in a safe and efficient way.

"They're not tour guides," she explained in a YouTube video. "Tour guides often have a lot of information and may need to be licensed. Greeters just want to meet people and share the city they love – people getting to know people, or from different cultures who might never meet each other."

Photo by Jermaine Ee at Unsplash

The local press picked up on Lynn's mission and so did national media, which worked to fuel the success of Big Apple Greeters.

Lynn's concept proved to be so effective that her vision of people helping people spread around the world to more than 100 cities where similar "Greeter" organizations were formed. The movement's popularity sparked creation of the International Greeter Association to form even more groups connecting volunteers with guests.

Before she died in 2013, Lynn envisioned the Greeter movement could contribute significantly to world peace simply because people were able to make friends around the country and the globe.

JIM BUTENSCHOEN

OFF TO BEAUTY SCHOOL AT AGE 57

For nearly a quarter century of grueling work in corporate sales and marketing, Jim Butenschoen lived an unfulfilled life. Sure, he was successful, but his life lacked purpose and meaning.

"Corporate became more important than customers. Internal processes and procedures, while important, were valued more than the needs of our clients. I really wanted to control my own destiny," he told Guidant Financial.

Jim invested nearly five years searching for the perfect business to buy. He wanted a turn-key operation rather than starting his own firm, so he decided to acquire a beauty salon. It certainly wasn't the type of industry he imagined entering, but he was attracted to the idea of growing a mom-and-pop business that trained others to become "salon ready" to help men, women and children look their best.

When he was 57 years old, Jim bought a salon and created the Career Academy of Hair Design. Since then, he has opened a total of five schools in Arkansas to accommodate steady growth.

He bought the school in 2006 just before the Great Recession, which proved to be a blessing. Jim learned when the economy is

Photo by Jason Leung on Unsplash

bad and people lose their jobs, that's when they go back to school, he told Fathers After 50.

"I love being my own boss and not being accountable to anyone other than myself," he said. "I have difficulty imagining my life without something going on or something I could do."

LORRAINE CAMPMAN

INSPIRING ADULTS TO MAKE MUSIC

Living in Pennsylvania, Lorraine Campman endured a series of office jobs that were not very satisfying. She got tired of reporting to bosses and having to do things their way. As she got older, Lorraine realized she needed to venture out on her own.

She loved music and worked as an independent piano teacher since 1977. However, Lorraine discovered her income-producing hours were limited to working afternoons when school ended and on weekends. That schedule really didn't create the life of freedom she desired.

In 2007, in her mid-50s, Lorraine took some entrepreneurial training classes, learned how to develop a business plan and got a start-up loan to launch Music Oasis Life Long Learning Center to teach older adults to play music. She was motivated to introduce her students to recreational music-making and teaching them to improvise.

Being a classically trained piano player, that required Lorraine to move out of her comfort zone to help others discover their own creativity.

Lorraine started teaching a class at her church with two side-by-side pianos. Unfortunately, six weeks after stepping out to pursue her dream, Lorraine was

Photo by Karol Carvalho at Pexels

diagnosed with breast cancer. That resulted in a two-year detour while she took care of her body and reclaimed her energy.

After recovering, Lorraine started teaching classes through her local community's recreation department before taking her training on the road to senior centers and retirement communities. Most of her students are retirement age, but want to fulfill a lifelong dream of learning to play music.

Lorraine acquired several digital pianos that enabled her to create portable music labs so students could sit at their own instruments while using headphones for privacy and to help with concentration. Eventually, she wanted to expand services to teach her methods to other instructors so they could inspire adults in their own communities to be creative as well.

"It is gratifying to me to see the range of people who have expressed interest in making music, have stuck with it and are enthusiastic about my program," Lorraine told Over50andOutofWork.com. "Don't let the music die inside of you. If you have a dream, then find a way of fulfilling that dream. Yes, there are going to be rough spots in the road along the way, but you have to persevere, accept available help and do what you can to make it happen."

JACK COVER

HIS ELECTRIFYING TOOL REVOLUTIONIZED LAW ENFORCEMENT

John Cover was born in Chicago in 1920 to highly-educated parents. His father was a professor of economics and his mother completed a master's degree in mathematics. So, it's no surprise that he was highly-educated himself.

Jack, as he preferred to be called, earned his doctorate in nuclear physics and went to work for the Naval Air Weapons Station after serving as an Army test pilot during World War II. For a while, he studied under the man who developed the world's first nuclear reactor. Jack also worked for IBM, Hughes Aircraft and even supported NASA's Apollo mission.

In 1970, when he was 50 years old, Jack developed a tool he hoped would help police officers avoid deadly confrontations, especially in hijacking situations where air marshals risked crashing a plane by firing bullets that could penetrate the walls and depressurize an aircraft.

Photo from Adobe Stock

Working from his garage, Jack's invention would propel tiny barbed darts attached to insulated wires at a subject. The handheld device would deliver up to 50,000 volts of pulsating electricity to cause muscle spasms and temporarily incapacitate a suspect.

He developed the concept after reading a story about a man who was immobilized after coming in contact with a live powerline, but survived. Jack called it a TASER, which stood for "Thomas A. Swift's

Electric Rifle," which was inspired by a childhood adventure book about a boy who invented a rifle that fired electricity.

According to Wikipedia, because the device used gunpower to propel darts, the federal government considered it a weapon that couldn't be sold to civilians, and law enforcement agencies were initially resistant to using it. Still, Jack received a patent for his invention in 1972.

The TASER gained popularity with a modified version he developed in 1993, at the age of 73, that used compressed air to fire darts instead. Because it was no longer considered a firearm, the TASER could be sold to the public, according to an article at www.beststungun.com.

The device is now standard equipment for police officers and prison guards around the world, and used by the military as well. Private citizens can also use a version of TASER for self-protection.

JULIA CHILD

HELPING AMERICANS FALL IN LOVE WITH FRENCH COOKING

Although she was technically 49 when her first book was published, Julia Child went on to have a major impact on the culinary arts until she died at 91.

Born in 1912 in Pasadena, Calif., Julia grew up in a family that hired a cook so she didn't prepare a meal on her own until after she was married in 1946.

However, just before that, Julia was credited for developing a "shark repellant" for the U.S. Navy during World War II. She experimented with a variety of concoctions that could be sprinkled in the water near underwater explosives to ward off sharks, which could accidentally detonate the naval mines.

After meeting her husband, Paul, the couple moved to Paris where he worked for the U.S. State Department. Looking for something to occupy her time, Julia enrolled in the Cordon Bleu cooking school and studied with master chefs.

Photo from Adobe Stock

Working with two women she met in France, Julia helped author a 726-page cookbook titled *Mastering the Art of French Cooking.* After the manuscript was rejected by one publisher for being too big, a smaller publishing company took on the project and the book became a runaway best seller.

Following her publishing success, Julia wrote articles for several magazines and even published a cooking column in the *Boston Globe*. She went on to publish 20 other books. Some were about her life, while most were centered on cooking.

Julia made a guest appearance on a TV show in Boston where she demonstrated how to properly make an omelet. That opened the door to her first television cooking show, *The French Chef*, when she was 51 years old. It was, perhaps, her greatest contribution to the cooking world. For more than 10 years, the program was broadcasting into homes, for which Julia won Peabody and Emmy awards.

A *New York Times* interviewer in 1990 mentioned criticism that her food wasn't very nutritional. Julia responded, "Everybody is overreacting. If fear of food continues, it will be the death of gastronomy in the United States. Fortunately, the French don't suffer from the same hysteria we do. We should enjoy food and have fun. It is one of the simplest and nicest pleasures in life."

BILL COUZENS

LAUNCHING A CHARITY AND NATIONWIDE BIKE RIDE TO END CANCER

As the COVID-19 problem was beginning to unfold in America and the rest of the world, Bill Couzens felt the nudge to begin a healthier lifestyle. So the 62-year-old Michigan resident bought the last electric bike in a shop he visited, the Traverse City *Record-Eagle* reported.

Bill's mother died of cancer, and so did his brother and sister. His sister's death from pancreatic cancer at age 50 motivated Bill to do something to help prevent cancer before it took its toll. His grief turned into purpose as Bill devoted his life to preventing losses like he experienced.

Bill doesn't just want to fight cancer, beat cancer or conquer cancer – he wants to stop it cold. So, he founded a charity called Less Cancer. He was the moving force behind creation of National Cancer Prevention Day on Feb. 4. He also worked with Children's Hospital of Michigan to educate families about the best ways to reduce cancer risks associated with environment and lifestyle.

Photo by Ahshea1 Media on Pexels

Perhaps his biggest undertaking was the Less Cancer Bike Ride America to raise money for his organization. It was a huge financial boost to Less Cancer. But, when COVID cancelled in-person events, Bill got creative and invited bicyclists to develop similar rides wherever they lived in the world. People from Mexico, Canada, France, Italy and many American states took part.

"I know what that pain feels like. That's a very real piece of my motivation for what I do — turning pain into power," he told the *Record-Eagle*. "Cancer is not supposed to be an expected stage of life. We're not treating cancer, but we're creating public health policies to help keep people from getting cancer."

MARY GRANVILLE DELANY

DEVELOPER OF PAPER COLLAGE

Born in 1700, Mary Granville had always been an artist, so she never stopped creating. As a widow at 72, she developed a new art form she called "paper mosaiks" (sic) that assembled a variety of individual shapes and colors to create a larger image.

Mary specialized in creating detailed and botanically-accurate plants by hand coloring pieces of tissue paper. She created nearly 1,000 unique pieces of art between the ages of 71 and 88 before her eyesight gave out. Her masterpieces are still on display at the British Museum in London.

With the support of King George III and Queen Charlotte, Mary was given a home to live in as well as a pension. In exchange, she taught children about plants as well as how to sew.

One publication, *The Life and Letters of Mary Granville* by C.E. Vulliamy, described her artwork this way:

"With the plant specimen set before her, she cut minute particles of colored paper to represent the petals, stamens, calyx, leaves, veins, stalk and other parts of the plant, and, using lighter and darker paper to form the shading, she stuck them on a black background.

Photo from Adobe Stock

"By placing one piece of paper upon another she sometimes built up several layers and, in a complete picture, there might be hundreds of pieces to form one plant. It is thought she first dissected each plant so that she might examine it carefully for accurate portrayal."

Living alone and well past the age women were expected to be contributing members to society, Mary developed and honed an art skill that people have imitated for centuries.

MARCIA DUHART

HELPING SENIORS MAKE SENSE OF TECHNOLOGY

Born in 1943, Marcia Duhart earned a degree in business administration from Rutgers University College in Newark, N.J. She eventually passed the 7-General Securities Representative Exam to become a corporate trainer for Merrill Lynch. Marcia later provided help desk support before rising to the position of assistant vice president of corporate training.

In 1999, she retired from the corporate world and founded her own company called CyberSeniors Services where Mary taught older people how to use the Microsoft Office suite of products, including Word, Excel, PowerPoint, Publisher and Outlook. She led her first classes at the Rossmoor adult community in Monroe Township, N.J., and other senior centers around the state.

Photo from Adobe Stock

According to Marcia's obituary, "...her entrepreneurship, creativity and energy opened a 21st century world of social networking to these seniors, who may not have gained these skills if not for Marcia."

The *New York Times* even featured Marcia for her ability to lead seasoned citizens on a path to computer literacy – something she had to figure out on her own.

"My business spread by word of mouth," Marcia explained, adding that some days demand was so great that she left home at 9 a.m. and returned at 7 p.m. "I've had students up to 90. I'm 67 now, and I have a lot of energy to do this because I do what I love – teaching people."

The economic downturn of 2008 hit Marcia hard. She lost much of her savings, which forced her to reduce expenses and take a part-time job working weekends as a receptionist at a local nursing home.

However, because she was able to provide essential computer training to other older adults, Marcia helped prepare them to work part-time jobs as well in order to weather the economic storm.

STEVE FINN

FORMER POLICE OFFICER HANGS UP HIS BADGE TO GIVE KIDS A SECOND CHANCE

As an Atlanta police officer, Steve Finn had seen too many young people make really poor decisions which sent them to jail for many years or, worse, to an early grave.

So the 51-year-old and his wife asked an all-important question, "Okay God, what do you want me to do with the time I'm here?"

Answers kept circling back to ways they could help kids who did not have hope or a future, he told *The Epoch Times*.

Steve went to work setting up Chestnut Mountain Ranch, a home that can accommodate 49 boys and teens in West Virginia. It provides help to youngsters from across America.

"We had enough money to keep our family fed for about a year," he told the paper. "I knew after 12 months, if we didn't have a plan, we would have to move back to Atlanta."

Photo from Adobe Stock

When Steve was down to his last $25, his faith was tested, but he did not give up — and that's when God showed up. Donations started pouring in and his dream soon became a reality.

"The boys we get have faced a lot of challenges. They didn't come here just to get their grades up," Steve explained. "They came here because of anger issues or broken families. Many of our children are in the foster care system."

Thanks to Chestnut Mountain Ranch, Steve helps the guys identify their purpose early in life and take steps to pursue it.

GERRY FIORGILIO

HELPING FAMILIES COPE WITH DEMENTIA

When Gerry Fiorgilio was 57, she had many years of experience as a registered nurse. But she had been laid off by several large corporations before approaching the Women's Opportunities Resource Center in Philadelphia for help in creating a five-year business plan and securing resources to launch her own company.

Gerry wanted to create a network of healthcare professionals who could provide homecare to elderly men and women, especially those who suffered from dementia.

In 2022, the Family Caregiver's Network included 80 homecare aides providing specialized round-the-clock care. The program is an alternative to nursing home placement by allowing patients to remain in the familiar surroundings of their own homes.

Gerry's staff also works with family members to help them identify and respond to caregiver burnout or depression. She created several support groups where caregivers can talk to others about the challenges and emotions surrounding providing care to dementia patients.

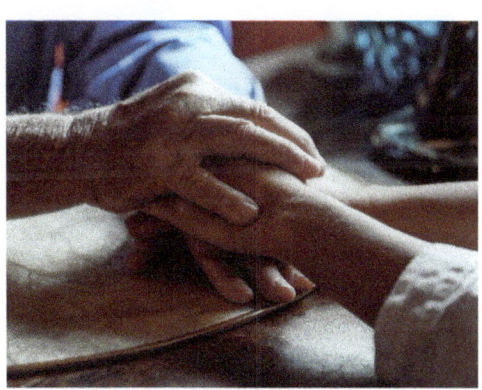

Photo by Kindel Media on Pexels

"Our patients have worked hard their whole lives, so it's important that they are relaxed for the next chapter. We specialize in connecting at-home live-in caregivers with seniors and families to bring quality eldercare home, where it belongs," she said.

With one in nine baby boomers expected to live into their 90s, Gerry's mission to train compassionate caregivers ensures her legacy will be helping others to preserve theirs.

LISA GABLE

THE GRANDMOTHER OF INVENTION

Like all women, especially those who frequently make presentations for work or engage in a lot of upper-body movement, Lisa Gable struggled with falling bra straps. Rather than complain, she went to work to solve the common problem by founding an intimate apparel company at the age of 70.

In 2003, Lisa invented the Strap-Mate, a device that hooks horizontally to the back straps of a woman's bra to prevent them from slipping off shoulders. It worked to fix her problem, but she wondered if others shared the same embarrassing situation.

So, Lisa surveyed 200 women and discovered a third of them were bothered by falling straps, according to a story in *Inc.* magazine. She patented her invention and decided to finance her new enterprise, L.G. Accessories, with personal credit cards. After all, who would give a 70-year-old woman a loan to start a new business?

Fortunately, Lisa had some business experience herself after working with her husband at an industrial chemical company founded by her parents. Those connections helped her find a local manufacturer and team up with a company to distribute the product nationwide. That enabled Lisa to land shelf space for Strap-Mate at Nordstrom, JCPenney and other specialty stores.

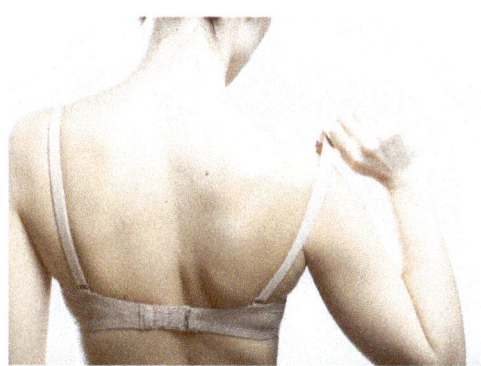

Photo from Adobe Stock

Over the years, Lisa's company expanded its product line to include a divided laundry bag for washing bras and other delicate garments. At one point, the Pennsylvania company generated $6 million in revenue and employed 30 people.

Even after entering her 84th year and breaking a hip twice, Lisa continued to work from home by checking up on order fulfillment and suggesting ideas for new products to her son, Steve, who managed day-to-day operation of the business.

Owning a business gave Lisa a great sense of pride and purpose in her later years by telling *Inc.* magazine, "If you have a reason to get up in the morning, that's the greatest reason to live."

CAROL GARDNER

A THERAPY DOG LED HER TO A FORTUNE

When she was 52, Carol Gardner found herself going through a divorce and deeply in debt. Depression set in and she saw no hope going forward. Her attorney told Carol to either see a therapist or get a dog. She chose the latter, a 4-month-old English Bulldog named Zelda.

The advice worked. Not only did Carol come out of the depression, she worked through her pain by starting a company to bring smiles to the faces of others. She partnered with a photographer who snapped pictures of Zelda wearing cute costumes and striking humorous poses.

Working from her living room, Carol penned cutesy sayings to accompany the photos and created 24 greeting cards which she marketed as Zelda Wisdom. She sold 1 million greeting cards within six months. After Carol and Zelda made appearances on some popular television shows, like *Good Morning America* and *Oprah*, her business exploded.

Later, she formed a partnership with the American Humane Society to train rescue dogs to live at children's hospitals where they help very sick kids and their families cope with the stress of life.

Photo by Camila Gomez on Unsplash

She has also published nearly a dozen books for children and adults to share more of Zelda's wisdom.

When life turned upside down for Carol, she thought outside her cage to bring joy and laughter to millions of people.

JOHN GLENN

THE FIRST AMERICAN TO ORBIT EARTH BECAME A U.S. SENATOR BEFORE HEADING BACK INTO SPACE

Some people might say John Glenn led a storied life. Born in 1921 in Cambridge, Ohio, John grew up in the Great Depression while his mother worked as a teacher and his father was a self-employed plumber.

When John was 8 years old, he flew in an airplane with his father, sparking a lifelong love of aviation. He built model airplanes out of balsa wood and sold rhubarb to buy his first bicycle, which he used to deliver papers. He was physically fit and played football, basketball and tennis during high school.

After starting college to study chemistry, John instead attained his private pilot's license before enlisting with the U.S. Navy as an aviation cadet. During advance training, he was invited to transfer to the U.S. Marine Corps and flew combat missions during World War II and the Korean Conflict.

Photo by NASA

That opened a door for him to become a test pilot who completed the first supersonic transcontinental flight in 1957. Already a minor celebrity, he became a household name after a profile was published in the *New York Times* and he appeared on *Name That Tune*.

When NASA started looking for America's first astronauts, John was selected as one of the original seven members of the Mercury program and was the first American to orbit earth. Now a national hero, he met John F. Kennedy and received a ticker-tape parade in New York City.

After an unsuccessful political campaign, John became the vice president of corporate development for Royal Crown International and bought a Holiday Inn hotel near the newly-opened Disney World resort when he was 52. He and his partner built three more hotels before John's career took a much different turn the next year after winning election to the U.S. Senate representing his home state of Ohio.

Although John tried unsuccessfully to run for president in 1984, he continued to serve as a U.S. senator until announcing plans to retire in January 1999 by claiming "there is still no cure for the common birthday." Yet, his career wasn't finished.

John returned to space aboard Space Shuttle Discovery when he was 77 years old to become the oldest person to enter earth orbit. For that feat, he received the Presidential Medal of Freedom in 2012 – four years before he died at the age of 95.

LEO GOODWIN

A GECKO'S GREAT GRANDFATHER

Born in 1886, Leo Goodwin began his career as an accountant in the insurance industry based in San Antonio, Texas, where he worked for the United States Automobile Association (USAA) to provide auto insurance to military members.

When he was 50, Leo changed the face of insurance by forming a company that bypassed agents and eliminated sales commissions by working directly with policyholders. Prior to that, auto insurance policies could only be purchased by working through an agent middleman.

With $25,000 of his own money plus another $75,000 investment and a vision for a better way to sell insurance, Leo founded the Government Employees Insurance Company, which later became known simply as GEICO. He envisioned a company that marketed policies to a narrowly-defined client group – federal employees – which enabled him to lower premiums and pass those savings directly to customers while still earning a profit.

Photo from Adobe Stock

At least that was his theory. Working side-by-side with his wife, Lillian, to build his dream, Leo moved the company to Washington, D.C., which had the largest concentration of federal employees. He worked 12-hour days to turn his vision into reality.

Leo did not take a salary for a number of years, opting instead to invest all profits back into growing his business. It was a slow process.

At the end of the first year, there were 3,700 policies in force and his company employed a dozen people. That meant GEICO operated in the red and was unable to cover all the costs associated with running the business. The firm did not recognize a profit until its fourth year in business.

However, in 1948, Leo decided to take the firm public after a mistake made while selling a portion of his company drew the attention of the U.S. Securities and Exchange Commission. That unfortunate turn of events may have been the best thing to happen to his firm.

When Leo retired in 1958, GEICO was worth $40 million. Many years after extending coverage to any licensed driver, not just federal employees, GEICO had $35 billion in revenue in 2020 and employed 40,000 people worldwide.

The firm's unofficial spokesman, a smart-alecky animated gecko named Martin, who speaks with a Cockney accent, is one of the most recognized brand icons in the world. The GEICO gecko owes his fame and fortune to the entrepreneurial vision of a man who died in 1971 – 28 years before the lizard was "born" for a 1999 ad campaign.

RUTH HANDLER

BARBIE'S INVENTOR CONTENDS WITH A SERIOUS PROBLEM

Born in 1916 in Denver to Jewish immigrants from Poland, Ruth Mosko later married Elliot Handler and moved to Los Angeles in 1938, where they formed a furniture business.

The Handlers later joined forces with Harold "Matt" Matson to launch a picture frame manufacturing company named Mattel Creations, and built dollhouses and doll furniture out of scrap lumber, Wikipedia noted.

When those houses proved to be more popular than picture frames, Mattel slowly transformed into a toy manufacturing firm. The company took an unexpected twist when Ruth designed an adultlike doll for her daughter, Barbara, who enjoyed playing with paper dolls, but imagined them as adults.

Photo from Adobe Stock

According to the Women Engineers Panel, Ruth realized children prefer imagining themselves as adults when playing and dreaming about the future. So, she crafted a three-dimensional doll that could wear clothing made from real fabric.

Ruth revealed the doll at the 1959 New York toy fair when she was 43 years old. By advertising on the *Mickey Mouse Club* TV show, sales of Barbie dolls skyrocketed to levels Ruth and her husband never imagined. Nearly 1 million dolls were sold that year.

However, in 1970, Ruth was diagnosed with breast cancer after turning 54 and required a radical mastectomy to save her life. At that time, there were few effective breast prostheses for cancer survivors. So, after being forced out of Mattel, Ruth created her own realistic prostheses made of liquid silicone enclosed in polyurethane. She added a rigid foam backing and called it Nearly Me.

Ruth formed Ruthton Corporation in 1976 to sell the device with right and left options based on bra size. She led a sales team of eight middle-age women, according to the *Washington Post*, and sold the devices in department stores. After Betty Ford underwent a mastectomy, Ruth personally fitted the former first lady with a Nearly Me.

By 1980, Ruthton surpassed $1 million in sales before it was sold to Kimberly-Clark Corporation. In 1997, Ruth was inducted into the Junior Achievement U.S. Business Hall of Fame.

ANGIE HIGA

FOUNDER OF SKY DREAMS

Angie Higa spent 30 years in the banking industry, but retired at age 48 to care for a grandchild while the youngster's mother was deployed to Afghanistan. One year later, when her family was planning a trip to welcome Angie's daughter stateside, she needed to fly to the reunion. Living in Hawaii, Angie would be on a red-eye flight and knew she needed a blanket because airlines stopped providing them.

Modifying a blanket her mother made as a gift when Angie was a teenager, she added a strap and pocket large enough to hold a neck pillow. After showing a friend what she created and receiving $1,000 worth of orders within a few weeks, Angie launched Sky Dreams in 2009 to keep up with demand.

She converted her garage into a workshop so Angie could continue to care for her grandchildren as well. She has since expanded her product line to cater to savvy and fashion-conscious travelers. Angie even encouraged her granddaughters to pursue their own dreams by helping them start an online business to sell hair accessories.

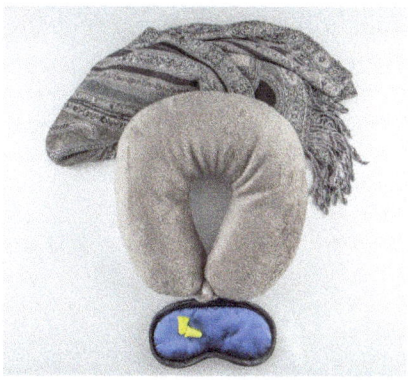

Photo from Adobe Stock

Although Angie was a few months shy of her 50th birthday when Sky Dreams was launched, she identified a problem, developed a creative solution to solve it and continued to pursue that purpose for more than 12 years.

DUNCAN HINES

A TRAVELING SALESMAN WITH A FONDNESS FOR GOOD CAKE

Working as a traveling salesman for a Chicago printer, Duncan Hines spent a lot of time on the road eating in restaurants and staying in hotels. That was long before the interstate highway system was completed and before big nationwide chains became commonplace.

Through that experience, Duncan became a real cake connoisseur.

At the age of 55, he and his wife, Florence, started assembling a list of recommended local restaurants for some friends. Duncan later turned that list into a profitable book. Then, he wrote a second book promoting his favorite local hotels and motels.

The books brought him a great deal of fame, which opened the door to writing a newspaper food column titled *Adventures in Good Eating at Home*. The syndicated column featured popular restaurant recipes adopted for home cooks. The column appeared three times a week.

Photo from Adobe Stock

In 1952, at the age of 72, he partnered with a New York bakery to market the Duncan Hines bread line. He sold the right to use his name to several food-related companies, which included a line of cake mixes that also bore his name.

Eventually, the cake mix business was resold to Proctor & Gamble in 1957, which made it a popular household brand in every state and expanded the line to include brownies, cookies and fruit pie fillings.

EDMOND HOYLE

MAKING CARD GAMES FAIR FOR ALL

Little is known about Edmond Hoyle because nobody really noticed him until he was 68 years old. That's when he expanded on his love for a card game called Whist.

He established formal rules for the game and wrote a paper explaining them. When he sold out of the initial pamphlet, Edmond sold the rights to his manuscript to a book publisher for what was a small fortune in 1742.

That prompted him to write rules for backgammon, chess, piquet, brag and quadrille. He also published a collection of rules for a variety of games, especially those involving gambling. Edmond was so influential in the gaming industry that he was inducted into the Poker Hall of Fame even though he died 60 years before that game was invented.

Edmond's books were translated into several languages and combined into one book that is still available today. *Hoyle's Rules of Games* made "according to Hoyle," an authoritarian phrase to keep games fair.

Photo by Alessandro Bogliari at Unsplash

ARIANNA HUFFINGTON

HELPING TO END EPIDEMIC OF STRESS AND BURNOUT

Born in Athens, Greece, Arianna wrote her first book at the age of 23 and ventured into conservative politics in her 40s. In 2005, at the age of 55, she co-founded *The Huffington Post*, an online news aggregation site that served as an outlet for news and commentary supporting issues from a more liberal perspective.

Photo from Adobe Stock

After selling the website to AOL for $315 million in 2011, Arianna resigned as editor-in-chief a short time later to launch Thrive Global to help people take control of their lives by offering new strategies and tools to address the unintended consequences of technology.

Her goal was to end a global epidemic of stress and burnout. Today, her company works with some of the largest firms in the world to promote employee well-being.

Now in her 70s, Arianna did not let age slow her down from continuing to make a worldwide impact.

JOHN & KATHY HUGGINS

LIVING THE RV DREAM

John and Kathy Huggins were lifted out of relative obscurity by a single idea to embrace a new hobby and teach others to join them on their journey.

Kathy had hinted for years that she wanted to go camping, so when they were 58 years old, the couple bought a great big tent, giant airbed and two sleeping bags just to try it out while attending a convention in Missouri. They loved the experience, but after a few nights of sleeping on the ground, the Huggins knew they were too old to do that again.

The trip prompted John and Kathy to attend a big RV show in Tampa in 2007. That's where they met people who enjoyed a full-time travel lifestyle by working part-time, temporary jobs around the country. When someone unexpectedly offered to buy their home, the Huggins bought a 39-foot motorhome and hit the road.

Photo from ForwardFrom50.com

The following winter, they were back in Florida visiting their sons when one of them asked the couple to host a weekly radio show, which they called *Living the RV Dream*. After 17 weeks, John and Kathy were ready to travel again, so they launched a podcast by the same name.

The Huggins started with 400 loyal weekly listeners, but that soon grew to 8,000 downloads every week. At that time, John and Kathy were encouraged to start a group on a relatively new social media platform called Facebook. In 2021, there were 82,500 active members.

In 2012, several people encouraged the couple to organize their podcast material into a reference book, which they did by writing "*So, You Want to be a Full-Time RVer?*" Then, in 2013, they wrote "*So, You Want to be a Workamper?*" After getting advice from another writer serving the RV community, the Huggins rewrote their original book and gave it a new title, "*So, You Want to be an RVer?*"

That was excellent advice because the Huggins sold tens of thousands of copies online and in bookstores. Camping World even stocked it in retail stores nationwide.

John remembers talking with people on the Living the RV Dream Facebook group who were always saying they were going to do it – someday.

"By the time they really decided to pursue their dream, they were in their 70s and too old to really enjoy themselves while traveling," he said. "So, do it now! Don't sit around and think about it or convince yourself you have to do something else first. You need to do it now! Your only regret will be not doing it 10 years earlier."

COLIN KING

HELPING CHILDREN GET SMARTER BY MAKING LEARNING FUN

Living in England, Colin King and his wife, Lisa, started Education Quizzes in 2012 when he was 58 years old.

His business concept was simple. He made education so much fun that children wanted to learn even when they were at home. The quizzes Colin wrote reinforced lessons students were taught in school.

What started as two-person project grew into an international company utilizing 28 writers to develop quizzes around subject matter for which they have formal training or specialized knowledge.

For $50 per year, parents, students and tutors have access to more than 3,000 quizzes and games designed for kindergarten-age students to high-schoolers, and even includes tests for Spanish and English as a second language. The website serves people in the United Kingdom, United States and India.

Photo by Julia M Cameron at Pexels

"People sometimes get mad with you while computers, tablets and phones never do – however many times you make the same mistake," Colin noted. "Schools are open for a few hours each day while this website will be there for you whenever you want it – 24/7."

RAY KROC

MAKING A FORTUNE FROM 15-CENT HAMBURGERS

Born in 1902 and raised near Chicago where he spent most of his life, Ray Kroc's early years were uneventful. He lied about his age in order to drive an ambulance with Walt Disney for the Red Cross during World War I when he was only 15 years old. According to Wikipedia, Ray's father had made a fortune on land speculation in the 1920s, but lost it all during the Great Depression.

Ray was also an entrepreneur at heart, even operating lemonade stands as a child, but he couldn't find his niche. He sold real estate and paper cups. He even played piano in local bands. Through his connections, Ray landed a job selling machines that could blend five milkshakes at a time to restaurants around the country.

Photo from Adobe Stock

Fate would take him to a restaurant in California which had placed an order for an unusually large number of mixers. It was there that he met Dick and Maurice McDonald who had devised a new way of making money by selling a very limited menu of items – hamburgers, cheeseburgers, French fries, milk shakes and soft drinks.

When Ray met the McDonald's brothers and saw their operation in person, he envisioned it could be franchised to other business owners as well. In 1955, when Ray was 53 years old, he agreed to become their franchising agent in exchange for a portion of the income he generated. At the time, hamburgers sold for 15 cents, fries were a dime and milk shakes were 20 cents, for which Ray earned 1.4% as the franchise agent.

This time, Ray's instincts were correct. Other business owners saw McDonald's potential as well and he helped open more than 100 restaurants within four years. A short time later, another Chicago-area businessman, Harry Sonneborn, suggested that in addition to taking a portion of hamburger sales, Ray should also develop a way to own the land upon which the restaurants were built. That way franchise owners must pay him monthly to lease the property.

Although that greatly improved Ray's ability to increase his income, the plan resulted in a falling out with the McDonald brothers. After buying out their interest in the restaurant in 1961, Ray turned McDonald's into a worldwide brand with more than 7,500 locations in 31 countries and generating $8 billion of annual revenue by the time he died in 1983.

By 2018, there were more than 37,000 McDonald's restaurants employing 210,000 people and generating $21 billion in revenue by serving 69 million customers daily.

With a personal fortune of more than $600 million, Ray retired from McDonald's in 1973 when he was 71 years old. He purchased the San Diego Padres baseball team the following year.

Ray also launched a charitable foundation with his third wife, Joan, which included establishing Ronald McDonald Houses near major medical facilities to allow sick children and their families to remain together during treatment.

SUNE LARSSON

PROVIDING OFFICE SPACE TO GROWING ENTREPRENEURS

For years, Sune Larsson bounced from one meaningless job to another until he turned 50. That's when he had an idea that changed his life. The Swedish entrepreneur would create an office space for new business owners who didn't have much money, but needed to appear successful while growing their companies.

The concept, called serviced offices, takes a floor of a professional building and divides it into individual suites, which are then used as offices. Some offices are fully furnished, and all the suites share common services. For example, renters use the same copier rather than buying an expensive machine themselves, and a receptionist answers phones or greets visitors for many independent companies.

Photo by LYCS Architecture on Unsplash

There is often a large conference room available for use by all tenants as well as central mail service, a common kitchen, etc. The offices enable business owners to claim an address in a prestigious business location without incurring 100 percent of the cost for rent, utilities, insurance, janitorial services and other staff.

Sune went all-in on his idea to help new businesses get off to the right start. He invested a big chunk of his savings and devoted much of his time to making it work. In an interview with *The Guardian* newspaper, Sune explained why success that seemed to elude him earlier in life finally caught up to him in his 50s.

"You don't have any small children at home anymore, so you don't have to sacrifice your time with your family and can concentrate on your business without having a bad conscience," he said. "The downside is that you have to keep fit and you can't be ill. You have to be there and find lots of energy, especially at the startup stage."

Freed from distractions, Sune created a successful business that provided income for him later when he eventually decided to slow down to enjoy even greater work-life independence.

OLIVE LYNCH

CREATING VALUE OUT OF WHAT'S VALUELESS

Formally trained as an opera singer and performer, when Olive Lynch decided she wanted a career change, she contemplated medicine and law before settling on studying computer technology and becoming a business analyst.

When Olive was unemployed for nine months during the Great Recession, rather than play video games all day, she started doing research on farming and organics, especially how it applied to composting. Through her research, the 52-year-old New Jersey resident developed a new technology for recycling food waste which transformed it into commodity products.

Photo from Adobe Stock

Food waste is a big concern for urban areas that either have limited landfill space or need to truck waste to other disposal sites. Food waste from supermarkets and food processing firms is often sent to composting operations. But, Olive found a way to make the waste even more useful and profitable. She formed a new company, Green Waste Technologies, to combat the problem.

Olive used the larvae of black soldier flies to consume food waste. Then, just before the insects pupate or enters a cocoon stage, the larvae are crushed to create an oil that can be used as a biofuel alternative to heating oil. It can also be made into protein meals for livestock. The process is superior to composting because biodigesters can help control methane.

She pitched her idea on *Sharkette Tank* before a dozen potential investors. Then, Olive presented her concept at the VANJ Pitching Olympics before even more investors where she came in 6th place. In itself, that feat is exceptional since research shows barely 10 percent of venture capital goes to women-owned companies.

"I have always liked to analyze. When faced with a problem, I don't have to solve it the way everyone else does. I'll look around and develop a different way," Olive said in an interview with Over 50 and Out of Work. "As a society we have a way we have always done things, and now we're facing the fact those ways aren't working. We can't solve problems by doing the same darn thing. We have to think of something different."

BERNIE MARCUS

FOUNDER OF HOME DEPOT

As a teenager, Bernie wanted to become a doctor, but his family could not afford tuition. So, he worked for his father making cabinets and eventually became a pharmacist. However, his true passion was in retailing merchandise rather than mixing drugs.

He worked in a variety of retail businesses before becoming the CEO of Handy Dan Improvement Centers. However, after Bernie was unceremoniously fired from the job in 1977 at the age of 49 during a corporate power struggle, he and a former co-worker founded Home Depot the next year.

Photo by Oxana Melis at Unsplash

According to Wikipedia, Bernie's company is the largest home improvement store in America today with more than 2,300 locations in the United States, Canada and Mexico. In fact, Home Depot helped push Handy Dan out of business in 1989.

With a net worth estimated at nearly $7 billion in 2021, Bernie went on to create the Marcus Foundation to provide financial support and resources for children, medical research, small businesses, military veterans, Israeli causes and general community needs.

When office politics tried pushing Bernie to the sideline, he didn't lay down and sulk. Instead, he turned his vision into an empire.

RANDALL MITCHELL

EQUIPPING TEENS WHO LEAVE FOSTER CARE

As Randall Mitchell was wrapping up his career with Verizon in 2008, the 52-year-old from Murchison, Texas, felt God calling him to start quilting, which was something he'd never done before.

After he retired, Randall and his wife, Charlene, got ready to sew and then waited for 16 years for more direction, WFAA-TV reported.

A letter from a young man provided the clarity Randall was seeking. Hunter Beaton, a 21-year-old college senior, started a charity called Day 1 Bags, to provide essential supplies to graduating high school seniors who were in the foster system and would soon be transitioning into a life of independence.

He asked Randall to make a quilt for each graduate – all 622 of them.

Tapping into a network of quilters, Randall reached the goal in nearly three months. Now 68 years old, he and his wife made four quilts themselves, and his network sewed 500 more.

Photo by Jeff Wade on Unsplash

Randall now believes his purpose is to give away just about every quilt he makes to someone who needs it.

"I said, 'God, you answered me through this this young man's email,'" Randall told WFAA. "And these kids are a big part of that answer."

TAIKICHIRO MORI

FROM COLLEGE INSTRUCTOR TO BILLIONAIRE LANDLORD

Born in 1904 in Tokyo, Japan, Taikichiro Mori's father was a well-to-do landlord. But, he did not want to follow in his father's footsteps. So, he went to college and became an instructor instead.

Taikichiro specialized in teaching trade theory, or how goods and services are moved within a country and internationally. From 1954 to 1959, he served as the dean of the College of Commerce at Yokohama City University.

After his father died in 1959, Taikichiro established the Mori Building Company to manage two buildings left to him in the estate. Although he was 55 at the time, Taikichiro wasn't content just managing those buildings. He started buying other commercial property around Tokyo.

Photo from Adobe Stock

Fate played a role as well. Demand for business locations was high, not only because Japan's economy was thriving, but foreign companies were scrambling for retail space to tap into the Japanese market.

He bought up single-home residential properties and erected high-rise buildings as residential and commercial complexes, according to a report in *Peoplaid*. The resulting buying frenzy made Tokyo's business district the most expensive real estate in the world.

As a result, 86-year-old Taikichiro became the richest man in the world in 1991 and 1992 with a net worth of $15 billion at the time, according to *Forbes* magazine.

GREG GERBER

ANNA MOSES

PURSUING HER CHILDHOOD PASSION FOR ART AT 78

The story of Anna Mary Robertson Moses proves people can make an impact well into their 70s. Affectionately referred to as "Grandma Moses," Anna started painting in earnest when she was 78 years old. She also refused to let her past define her future.

She was born in 1860, five years before the Civil War ended. She started working as a live-in housekeeper at the age of 12 and continued to do that for 15 years until she married one of the other farm workers. She and her husband worked a variety of farm jobs for almost 20 years before buying a farm of their own.

Only five of their children survived infancy and Anna's husband died of a heart attack when she was 67. She continued to operate the farm with her son for another nine years before moving to her daughter's home.

Anna nurtured an interest in art since she was a teenager. That's when an employer noticed her fascination with a Currier and Ives painting and gave Anna chalk and wax crayons to create her own art. She also loved embroidery, until arthritis forced an end to that hobby when she was 76.

Photo from the U.S. Bureau of Engraving

Anna's sister suggested she pursue her childhood dream of painting. At that point, Anna was an unknown artist.

But, she loved to paint scenes of rural life and New England landscapes. Anna wanted to capture those moments so future generations would know how her generation lived at the time.

Despite being an octogenarian, Anna completed 1,500 paintings, which she sold for up to $5 per canvass. As her fame grew, her paintings grew in value. In fact, one sold for $1.2 million in 2006 and another was featured as a postage stamp in 1969 – eight years after her death – and is on display at the White House.

Grandma Moses proves you're never too old to embrace your passions and influence people for generations in the process.

CLARA PELLER

ENJOYING A BEEFY CAREER AS AN ACTRESS AT 81

A manicurist for more than 35 years, Clara Peller lived most of her life in the Chicago area. When she was 80 years old, hard of hearing and suffering from emphysema, Clara was hired to provide manicures for a company filming a television commercial at a local barbershop.

With her no-nonsense demeanor and a unique voice, Clara started performing in several commercials. She was especially well known for her role as a cleaning lady in an advertisement promoting the Megabucks game for Massachusetts State Lottery.

But that experience paled in comparison to the fame she received in 1984 working for the Wendy's fast-food chain. Cast in a trio of elderly women who were served hamburgers in a big bun, but with a tiny meat patty, Clara demanded to know "Where's the beef?"

Photo from Adobe Stock

The three-word phrase became a cultural phenomenon, according to Wikipedia. Within a year, Wendy's sales jumped 31% worldwide. The phrase was even uttered by former vice president Walter Mondale during his unsuccessful presidential campaign in 1986.

"With Clara, we accomplished as much in five weeks as we did in 14.5 years," said Denny Lynch, Wendy's senior vice president for communications.

She was paid a total of $500,000 for her work on the commercial and subsequent product tie-ins, then went on to star in several more advertisements for other companies. Clara even made an appearance on *Saturday Night Live.*

JOHN STITH PEMBERTON

HIS FIZZY WATER CONCOCTION BECAME A WORLDWIDE SENSATION

Born in 1831 in Knoxville, Ga., John Stith Pemberton earned his medical degree at the age of 19. After practicing medicine and performing surgery for a while, he eventually opted to open a drug store in Columbus, Ga., before joining the Confederate Army and rising to the rank of lieutenant colonel.

John suffered a saber wound to his chest during the battle of Columbus and soon became addicted to morphine to control pain. Seeking to end his addiction, John experimented with a variety of pain-relieving compounds he thought would provide an alternative to the popular, but highly-addicting drug.

According to Wikipedia, his first recipe was called "Dr. Tuggle's Compound Syrup of Globe Flower," which was derived from a toxic plant called the buttonbush. Later, he tried combining coca and coca wines before stumbling on a formula which mixed kola nut extracts with the damiana plant. He called that alcoholic beverage "Pemberton's French Wine Coca."

Photo from Adobe Stock

John's "medicine" was popular among war veterans and ladies, especially "all those whose sedentary employment causes nervous prostration," Wikipedia noted. However, when some regions of Georgia enacted temperance legislation outlawing alcoholic drinks, he had to concoct a non-alcoholic version.

In 1886, when John was 55 years old, he solicited the help of another Atlanta drugstore operator named Willis E. Venable to help him perfect the secret formula to a new beverage. By accident, he mixed a base syrup with carbonated water to create a delicious drink he sold in soda fountains.

Frank Robinson, who worked as an early marketing expert, came up with the name Coca-Cola, which was a play on the beverage's two main ingredients, the coca plant and kola nut. Although John claimed his product was a valuable brain tonic that could cure headaches, relieve exhaustion and calm nerves, he marketed it as a drink that was "delicious, refreshing, pure joy, exhilarating and invigorating."

Still battling a morphine addiction and stricken by stomach cancer two years later, John sold his portion of the Coca-Cola patent to his business partners for what was the equivalent of $50,000 today. In 2020, John's product was available in more than 200 countries and the Coca-Cola company achieved more than $33 billion in sales.

DEBORAH RAMSEY

MASSAGING A NEW BUSINESS AND CAREER AT 52

After entering the working world right out of high school, Deborah Ramsey navigated through a series of layoffs, promotions and job changes with banks, insurance companies and consulting businesses.

In 2005, when she was 52 years old and facing the prospect of another layoff, the Philadelphia native knew it was time for her to make a change to have better control over the direction of her life.

"I had been through two big layoffs before and I knew what they smelled like," she told *Fox Business*.

Photo from Adobe Stock

Deborah also had additional responsibilities at home taking care of a disabled daughter, her aging mother and mother-in-law, as well as her husband, who was a disabled veteran. Through those experiences, Deborah developed an interest in herbal remedies and massage therapies.

Because she enjoyed receiving massages herself, and sensing that women over 50 also needed to start relaxing and taking better care of themselves, Deborah went back to school to become a professional massage therapist.

She launched a practice in her basement. It grew quickly and she rented storefront space where Natural Wellness and Spa was born. Deborah received a $35,000 start-up loan to cover the cost of moving and training.

"We've moved from a focus on pampering and relaxation to a medical orientation. We're doing natural treatments for things like fibromyalgia and arthritis, and weight reduction for older women," she told *Fox Business*. "That's where the money is. I'm doing more now than I could have ever imagined. I don't know why I didn't do this sooner."

PETER MARK ROGET

HIS WAY WITH WORDS MADE COMMUNICATION EASIER

Born in London in 1779, Peter Mark Roget was a physician and natural theologian who enjoyed a fascination with words. When his medical career got off to a slow start, he shifted gears and tutored the sons of a prominent British manufacturer.

He eventually returned to medicine and gave lectures on physiology, or the study of how organisms work to carry out chemical and physical functions in a living system. He also helped found the University of London in 1837 at the age of 58.

Shortly after his 60th birthday, Peter retired and began working on his legacy project that continues today. He developed an obsession with list making as a child – a skill that would prove to be beneficial much later in his life. In an effort to battle depression, he maintained a notebook of words which he organized by their meaning.

Photo from Adobe Stock

In 1852, at the age of 73, Peter published his catalogue of words in a book he titled "*Thesaurus of English Words and Phrases Classified and Arranged so as to Facilitate the Expression of Ideas and Assist in Literary Composition.*" The book was later known simply as Roget's *Thesaurus*.

Before the book rights were sold in an auction, Peter's son and grandson continued to revise and expand the catalogue which remains an invaluable resource for English writers, journalists and editors.

COLONEL HARLAND SANDERS

BUILDING A LEGACY ON HIS FINGER-LICKIN' GOOD RECIPE

Harland Sanders, a white-haired southern gentleman born in 1890 who capitalized on the phrase "finger lickin' good," did not even discover his purpose until he was 62 years old.

Before then, he worked a plethora of jobs, including as a blacksmith's helper, railroad fireman, lawyer, life insurance salesman, ferry boat owner, lamp manufacturer, tire salesman, service station attendant, motel operator and cafeteria manager.

Photo from Adobe Stock

Fired from multiple jobs for insubordination and brawling, Harland was 45 when he received an honorary commission as a colonel from the governor of Kentucky.

Shortly after turning 50 in 1942, he finalized a secret recipe to cook chicken in a pressure cooker rather than a frying pan. Harland franchised his first restaurant at the age of 62 when, according to Wikipedia, he had meager savings and lived on a $105 monthly check from Social Security.

Within 10 years, there were more than 600 Kentucky Fried Chicken locations throughout the United States, Canada and Mexico. He sold the company for $2 million in 1964 and became the company's brand ambassador by traveling more than 200,000 miles annually to promote the chain.

Before his death in 1980, the colonel established a charitable organization to help fund the operation of children's hospitals and other charities. Valued at $3.5 million, the foundation still donates up to $500,000 per year to various causes.

Harland may have struggled to find his true calling for most of his life. But at an age when many people are looking to retire, rather than lay around twiddling his thumbs, Harland licked his fingers and turned his secret recipe into a worldwide phenomenon.

JUDITH SHEINDLIN

HERE COMES THE JUDGE

The daughter of a dentist and stay-at-home mother, Judith Sheindlin was born in 1942 and grew up comfortably in New York City before attending college in Washington, D.C., where she earned a degree in government. From there, she returned to the Big Apple to attend law school.

For two years after passing the bar, Judith worked as a corporate lawyer for a cosmetics company. Then, she left the workforce to raise her young son and daughter. Once they reached school age, Judith went to work for the New York family court system where she presided over cases involving child abuse, domestic violence and juvenile crime.

Her no-nonsense approach to meting out justice helped her become a supervising judge in the Manhattan family court system. Her reputation led to an article in the *Los Angeles Times* profiling her as a woman determined to make courts work for the common good, according to Wikipedia. That article led to a *60 Minutes* segment which brought her national recognition.

Photo from Adobe Stock

In 1996, at the age of 54, Judith wrote a book titled *"Don't Pee on My Leg and Tell Me It's Raining"* in which she highlighted some of the tragic cases she presided over in family court. It still ranks in Amazon's Top 20 books about the legal profession.

However, it was her *60 Minutes* appearance which opened the door to an opportunity that would make her a household name.

As Judge Judy, she presided over televised small claims cases for 25 years to an audience of nearly 10 million people every day. Her show ranked at the top of Nielsen ratings for court programming and was often the highest-rated show for daytime television. She was nominated for an Emmy Award more than 15 times and won three of the awards.

Because of her popularity, Judith earned $900,000 per workday for the 52 days a year she taped episodes, making her the highest-paid TV star, according to *TV Guide*.

ERNESTINE SHEPHERD

WORLD'S OLDEST FEMALE BODYBUILDER AT 85

It is impressive to be listed in the *Guinness Book of World Records* for anything, but it's incredible to be honored for being the world's oldest female bodybuilder.

Ernestine Shepherd didn't set foot inside a gym until she was 56 years old. "I was always too prissy to work out – and you couldn't get me away from chocolate cake," she told *Madamenoire*.

Her attitude changed that year after she and her sister went shopping for swimsuits and decided some lifestyle changes were overdue.

Photo from Adobe Stock

Following her sister's sudden death from a brain aneurism and a brief bout of depression, Ernestine forged ahead to pursue the weight training goals they had set for themselves. She worked hard enough to risk entry into a body-building competition for which she placed first in her age group.

At 85, Ernestine said she really doesn't need an alarm clock to wake her up at 2:30 a.m., which she considers the ideal time to begin her daily devotions. After a breakfast of 10 scrambled egg whites, a few walnuts and a bottle of water, she's ready to embrace a new day.

Despite her age, Ernestine even taught a weight training class for women and men who want to get into shape.

FOUJA SINGH

SETTING RACE RECORDS STARTING AT AGE 89

When he was born in 1911, Fouja Singh was so weak that he did not walk until he was nearly 5 years old. As a result, he was often teased in his youth and nicknamed "danda," which means "stick," well into his teens. As a young man, he was an avid runner who gave it up to become a farmer in India.

After the untimely deaths of his wife, son and daughter in the early 1990s, Fouja sank into a depression and moved to England to live with one of his sons. According to *Religion News*, he would pass the days by watching television in his living room. One day, he watched the London Marathon and felt inspired to take up running again.

He started training when he was 81 years old and entered his first marathon eight years later in 2000. When he was 93, Fouja finished a 26-mile marathon in 6 hours 54 minutes, which broke the world record for the over-90 age group by nearly an hour.

Nicknamed the Turbaned Tornado, Fouja set five world running records in one day after turning 100. He became the first person to ever complete a marathon after passing the century mark. He crossed the finish line for Toronto's Waterfront Marathon in 2011 in 8:25:17 – and that was after it took 14 minutes for him to reach the starting line.

Photo from Adobe Stock

Fouja was one of the torchbearers for the London Summer Olympics in 2012 and received the British Empire Medal for meritorious civil service in 2015. Joining three other Sikhs aged 79 and 80, they formed the running group Sihks in the City and ran in the Edinburgh Marathon.

Weighing in at 115 pounds, Fouja attributes his physical fitness and longevity to abstaining from smoking and alcohol while following a simple vegetarian diet of phulka, dal, green vegetables, yogurt and milk. He refuses to eat rice or any other fried food.

When Fouja retired from running in 2012, he held every running-related record for men over the age of 100 for events ranging from 100 meters to a marathon, the last of which he completed at 101 – a record many people predict will survive for years to come.

As of 2019, the 108-year-old still advocated for healthy living and continued walking five miles a day around his London neighborhood.

SAM TAYLOR

COMBINING A PASSION FOR BUSINESS WITH A LOVE FOR ART

When Sam Taylor retired at 63 years of age, he was already on top of his game. He made plenty of money over the years in business and was looking forward to retiring to a villa in southern Spain.

Yet, he wasn't retired for long when Sam realized something was drastically missing from his life – purpose. He tried his hand as an angel investor who provided funding for start-up companies in return for a slice of future profits. He also served as a director on the boards for other businesses in his native Scotland.

Sam was eight years into retirement when he discovered a way to turn his passion for business into a profitable online venture of his own.

His wife, who was five years younger than Sam, had been creating art out of textiles, according to *The Guardian* newspaper. Sam realized that his wife could greatly expand her customer base by setting up an online art gallery and attracting customers from all over the world.

Photo from Adobe Stock

Eventually, the site sold not only his wife's art, but pieces created by 30 other Scottish artists as well. While some people might say older people are out-of-touch when it comes to navigating online technology, Sam knew he possessed the business experience and, more importantly, the connections it would take to get his own fledgling firm off the ground.

"What you bring to the party at that age is your experience and contacts," he told *The Guardian*. "To us, age is no barrier at all. If you're mentally alert and physically fit, there's no reason why you can't do it."

MARY TENNYSON

FOUNDER OF STASHALL

A tragic situation for Mary Tennyson paved the way to a lucrative career by addressing a need among seasoned citizens with mobility issues.

Mary's 87-year-old mother fell and broke her hip, which required her to use a walker to move from place to place. However, the fashion-conscious woman liked to carry large purses with her to store everything women want to keep close at hand. However, the big bags worked to throw her off balance, which posed a serious safety issue.

"All Mom wanted was something for the front of the walker that would replace her bag and match her outfits," Mary told AARP.

After scouring department stores for a walker-friendly purse and coming up empty handed, Mary decided use an old sewing machine to make one for her mother.

Her mom loved the gift, and all her friends offered compliments on the design and functionality. Soon, Mary had lots of orders for other bags.

She created the StashAll line to manufacture and distribute the products. Mary sought assistance

Photo from Adobe Stock

from the Service Corps of Retired Executives (SCORE), which is managed by the U.S. Small Business Administration.

Sold in a variety of fashionable designs, the sturdy bags are made in California from different materials, including fabric, synthetic leather and even bark cloth.

"I don't want to get stuck working full time again," Mary told AARP. "I'm not so driven that I want to go from my desk to my grave."

JULIE WAINWRIGHT

PERSONAL FAILURES FUEL A BUSINESS THAT GENERATED $500 MILLION IN SIX YEARS

In November 2000, Julie Wainwright faced divorce and the demise of an online business for which she had invested her heart and soul for years.

The combination pushed her into a dark period of her life where she didn't have much motivation to do anything other than paint and workout. She did accept a job at a venture capital firm, but felt uninspired, a profile at *CNBC* revealed.

Julie remembers having a conversation with a girlfriend and saying, "Man, this could be a really bad second half of my life, or I have to figure something out. I had never created my own business before. But I had to finally say, nobody is going to give me my dream job, so I better figure it out myself."

After speaking with another friend who liked to buy secondhand luxury clothes from trusted stores,

Photo from Adobe Stock

and knowing Julie had a closet full of items herself that could be resold as well, the conversation was an inspirational moment for her. The former CEO of Pets.com, Julie understood how ecommerce worked; however, the challenge would be to create a venue that couldn't be duplicated by Amazon.

Julie was in her mid-50s when she launched The RealReal in March 2011. The website specialized in selling secondhand luxury items that were consigned by others. The firm would arrange to pick up items at a seller's home, confirm their authenticity and then ship them to buyers.

One year later, The RealReal surpassed the $10 million mark in sales. That "minor" success helped generate $173 million in venture capital from 22 investors. By 2017, the company enjoyed $500 million in revenue and employed 950 people, according to *CNBC*.

By 2022, after the company started trading stock, Julie had opened 16 physical retail stores in swanky locations across the country. She was also instrumental in getting the first Monday of October designated as National Consignment Day.

"Failure is ultimately very liberating," Julie said. "Once you come out the other side of it, you just might have faced one of your biggest fears and lived. The other side of failure is a big elimination of fear of failure. Trust me, that is an amazing gift."

MICHELLE WEIDENBENNER

HELPING A MILLION MOMS CLOSE THE GAP BETWEEN HAVOC AND HOPE

For many years, Michelle Weidenbenner made draperies and dabbled in interior design while her husband, Dave, traveled extensively for work. The couple had two biological children, a girl and boy, but she felt called to adopt another child.

So, they adopted a girl from Russia who was developmentally delayed and required a bit more attention. The baby was also more than 11 years younger than her older brother and sister, so Michelle became a stay-at-home mom.

Closing in on 50 and still raising a young child, Michelle took up writing to keep her mind sharp. She took courses and attended conferences to meet other writers, but she did not publish anything.

When Michelle was nearly 60, she and her husband became guardians of their two elementary-age granddaughters when their parents became homeless after addiction took a tremendous toll on their lives. Now a stay-at-home grandmother, Michelle started writing about her experiences and has since published nine books.

Photo from Forward From 50

One of her books was a novel that delved into reactive attachment disorder, a problem common among children who spent time in institutions. She also wrote a series of children's books to help kids develop coping mechanisms for dealing with serious problems, like an alcoholic parent. She even co-wrote a book with her 7-year-old granddaughter.

Michelle's first non-fiction book, "*Unhackable Moms of Addicted Loved Ones: Closing the Gap Between Havoc and Hope*," was written to encourage mothers trying to help their loved ones overcome addiction.

She founded the All Mighty Moms tribe and launched the Moms Letting Go Facebook group to create a support community for people who had read the book. Her podcast offers advice from people who've already lived through a family addiction problem.

"My book is specifically written for moms of addicted loved ones who want to heal from the shame, blame and chaos so they are in a better position to help their children and others," said Michelle. "It's a 30-day program which takes readers through a healing process. There will be a self-help course moms can take, and they'll have the option to become a certified coach and implement this program in their own communities.

"This is the No. 1 thing that just lights my soul on fire. My goal is to empower a million moms of addicted loved ones to get into recovery by 2025," Michelle explained "I know I can't fight the problem by myself. But with a million mama bears joining me, we can really help transform recovery options, jails and prisons, and our families."

THOMAS WEST

SELLING COFFEE TO HELP VETERANS, FAMILIES TRANSITION TO CIVILIAN LIFE

Military service can be strenuous. There are lots of deployments where soldiers, sailors and airmen are separated from their families for long periods of time. They're also deployed into situations that can cause post-traumatic stress disorder (PTSD) after returning home.

Thomas West understands how they feel. The 52-year-old from Williams, Ariz., is a U.S. Marine Corps veteran himself. He personally experienced the struggles of coming home and adjusting to civilian life, dealing with homelessness, alcoholism, PTSD and broken relationships.

He formed Operation Transition Outside the Wire, a non-profit, veteran-owned company. Thomas plans to develop 130-acres for a ranch to house veterans and their families up to six months while they transition from military to civilian life.

During their time at the ranch, veterans and their spouses will be offered housing, employment, transitional support services, transportation, community and resources to help with job searches, higher education and whatever other needs that come up, an article in the *Williams-Grand Canyon News* reported.

Photo from Adobe Stock

It's a vital service, but it costs money to provide. Thomas can't count on the government for support because they won't fund any programs offering help to veterans plus their families and children. But, he feels it is essential that everyone work together to make a successful transition.

So, Thomas' mission is funded entirely by the sale of its specially-blended Operation Transition Outside the Wire coffee. The beans are grown on private plantations in Guatemala and Nicaragua, then roasted in Williams and sold on the organization's website.

"By partnering with corporations, private donors and other non-profits who believe in and support our mission, we strive to prevent as many of the 22 veteran suicides that occur every day," he explained. "This gives them the necessary time to develop their new purpose."

LAURA INGALLS WILDER

MEMORIALIZING HER FAMILY'S DIFFICULT PRAIRIE LIFE

Born in 1867 in a Wisconsin log cabin, Laura Ingalls moved out of the big woods with her family when she was 2 years old to settle in Indian country near Independence, Kansas.

When she was a child, her family faced a number of tribulations including wildfires, eviction, severe drought, failed crops, illness and early death as they traveled to many Midwestern states via a covered wagon while her father looked for work or tried to establish a farm.

To help her family make ends meet when she was 15 years old, Laura took a job as a teacher in a one-room school before getting married a year later. Laura and her husband tried farming in several locations before she landed a job as a newspaper columnist at the age of 44. Combined with farming, Laura's writing kept her family afloat for many years.

Photo by Acton Craword at Unsplash

But, the stock market crash of 1929 financially wiped out the family. The death of Laura's mother and older sister prompted her to preserve those childhood memories. The collection of stories was eventually turned into a book titled *Little House in the Big Woods* and published in 1932 when Laura was 65 years old.

The harrowing novel proved to be wildly successful and encouraged Laura to write *Little House on the Prairie* and several others. By the time of her death in 1957, three days after Laura's 90th birthday, her books had become childhood favorites inspiring generations of boys and girls throughout the world.

MARY JANE WILLIAMS

FROM HOMESCHOOLING MOM TO REAL ESTATE INVESTOR

Prior to turning 50, Mary Jane Williams was a homeschooling mother of six living in Fort Myers, Fla. Today, her granddaughter is an ideal playmate for Mary Jane's youngest son, who is just one year younger.

Her family had been full-time RVing for five years before Mary Jane learned she was expecting. The happy news took the family off the road until the boy was born. Then they started traveling again for a few more adventures before opting to buy a hobby farm while her husband continued to work his remote technology job.

Photo from ForwardFrom50.com

After turning 50, Mary Jane ventured into rehabilitating and flipping homes with a business partner. They buy homes, fix them up and their either resell or rent them to others. She had no experience in flipping homes when she decided to pursue the opportunity. At first, Mary Jane and her husband simply purchased land, held it for a bit and resold it for a profit.

When advancing technology threatened to bring his career to a halt, Mary Jane saw house flipping as a way to match her husband's current income to give their family more options. Then providence stepped in and connected her to a son's friend who had been flipping homes for years.

"It was an ideal combination," said Mary Jane. "He had all the knowledge and know-how needed to flip homes successfully, and we had the financial assets to enable us to acquire properties and supplies. So we teamed up on a few projects and work very well together."

The couple had been sitting on a vacant home that once belonged to his grandparents. When they decided to sell the waterfront home, the Williams realized just how sizeable an investment it was. Not only would the original home bring a nice price, but the lot could be divided into two additional lots – each of which would be very attractive to homebuyers.

By selling the home and lots, the Williams received a sizeable amount of money, which enabled them to buy more homes to flip. Through the process of selling several flip homes, a few people approached her to see if they had any homes for rent. With home prices skyrocketing, there was significant demand for rental units.

For people contemplating what to do after turning 50, Mary Jane advises them to focus on one thing they think they'd like to do and then learn all they can about it.

"YouTube is wonderful. You can become YouTube-certified in just about anything," she explained. "The important thing is to keep gathering knowledge."

GREG GERBER

A SERIAL DREAMER WHO WOULDN'T GIVE UP

By the time Greg Gerber got married at 24, he already had nearly 20 jobs working in restaurants, law enforcement, and the military. Yet, he always hungered for something more.

He enjoyed success as a newspaper editor in the U.S. Air Force, but Greg knew the military regiment wasn't for him. A relative encouraged him to start a photography business in New Mexico, which grew quickly as he took pictures at high school dances, weddings, sports team and college parties.

Photo by Denu Photography

Greg was recognized as the fastest growing event photographer in America in 1988, and bankrupt a year later. His business had grown much faster than his ability to manage it. After his wife learned she was pregnant with their third child and was determined to move closer to family in Wisconsin, Greg agreed to shut down the business and follow them.

He returned to college to complete a degree in public relations, but still struggled to find the ideal job. He worked for several local newspapers, two non-profit organizations and even sought to launch an indoor family entertainment center.

Then Greg stumbled into a job as a journalist covering the recreation vehicle industry, which required extensive travel around the country, but meant he was frequently away from his family. After the publishing company he worked for had been sold several times and the new owners didn't understand how the internet would dramatically impact their business, Greg and a co-worker partnered with another firm to launch a new magazine.

The Great Recession wasn't the ideal time to begin a new project that relied on advertising. That publishing company folded and Greg found himself out of work one year later. His marriage, which had been on shaky ground for years, collapsed shortly after his youngest daughter moved out of the house.

After losing everything he had worked to build, Greg moved to Arizona to live rent-free at a relative's home. He started his own online business providing news and information about the RV industry, as well as launching the first podcast devoted to the business side of the RV market.

He enjoyed success for several years before deciding to buy a motorhome and tour the country while interviewing RV dealers, manufacturers, suppliers, campground owners and RV owners. Thinking it would be the pinnacle of his career, it turned out differently.

Greg wrote a series of editorials outlining many troubling aspects about the industry from product quality, lack of repair services, limited campground space, etc. While well received by RV owners and most people working in the industry, he irritated a very large manufacturing conglomerate that pressured Greg's advertisers to discontinue their support.

He eventually shut down the publication to pursue a new business as a faith-based writer and author. But, reeling from the effects of burnout, Greg struggled to gain traction. He also suffered a mild stroke the following year, which was demotivating. Greg was puzzled about what he was supposed to do. It was a familiar feeling.

"I remember spending some quiet talking about it with God. I was overcome with this feeling of God saying, 'Didn't we discuss this a few years ago? I want you to be using your skills to help other people,'" Greg explained.

But, he still had no idea what he was supposed to do to "help other people." Living alone in Arizona with his family scattered around the country, loneliness and depression took hold. Then COVID upended the entire world, which only worked to exacerbate the problem.

Fortunately, Greg had some freelance writing assignments which helped pay the bills. However, he still felt called to do more, but what?

One afternoon in late 2021, while discussing the situation with a mentor, Greg realized he wasn't alone. Many people over the age of 50 have the same problems where they are forced out of jobs they love, or working in jobs that leave them uninspired. They might be separated from their families and feeling there has to be more to life than the dreary existence they're living.

From that conversation, Forward From 50 was born. Greg had renewed energy to help men and women over the age of 50 who, just like him, want to enjoy purposeful lives by pursuing things they're passionate about. As soon as he took one step of faith toward his new purpose, things started falling into place.

"It's truly amazing how quickly someone can become depressed and hopeless when they dwell upon the negative aspects of their situation," Greg said. "There is an old saying that a person can live 40 days without food, four days without water and four minutes without oxygen, but not even four seconds without hope."

He built an online community to connect with seasoned citizens who wanted to find and pursue life-giving purpose. He set up a podcast to inspire others by allowing people to share their experiences in their own words. Greg is also developing online training classes to help people establish a success path to enjoy a fulfilling purpose in the second half of their lives.

"People love stories, especially inspirational ones about how others overcame adversity to achieve their goals," he explained. "Often all people need to become successful at anything is knowing that since someone else could do it, then they can, too."

For more inspirational stories of men and women over the age of 50 who have found purpose by passionately pursuing things they're interested in, visit www.forwardfrom50.com and subscribe to the free *Moving Forward* weekly newsletter.

RESOURCES

Pages	Profile	Resource
1-2	Richard Adams	https://en.wikipedia.org/wiki/Richard_Adams
3-4	Momofuko Ando	https://en.wikipedia.org/wiki/Momofuku_Ando
5-6	Dave Bateman	https://www.hawaiibusiness.com/entrepreneurs-after-age-50; https://www.nfib.com/content/news/start-a-business/nfib-member-profile-how-corporate-burnout-produced-a-successful-coffee-farmer-72733/
7-8	Harry Bernstein	https://en.wikipedia.org/wiki/Harry_Bernstein; https://en.wikipedia.org/wiki/The_Invisible_Wall_(memoir); https://www.southcoasttoday.com/story/lifestyle/2007/04/03/96-year-old-proves-it/52935819007/
9-10	Janet Black	https://www.forwardfrom50.com/blog/janet-black-using-personal-pain-to-bring-comfort-to-others/

Pages	Profile	Resource
11-12	Wally Blume	https://www.mlive.com/business/west-michigan/2015/02/michigan_entrepreneurs_story_f.html; https://www.denaliingredients.com/history/; https://cbn.com/700club/features/Amazing/Blumes081205.aspx
13-14	Lynn Brooks	https://internationalgreeter.net/greeter-idea/lynn-brooks; https://www.bigapplegreeter.org/history-mission
15-16	Jim Butenschoen	https://www.guidantfinancial.com/success-stories/career-academy-of-hair-design/
17-18	Lorraine Campman	https://overfiftyandoutofwork.com/blog/older-entrepreneurs-lorraine-campman/
19-20	John Cover	https://en.wikipedia.org/wiki/Taser; https://en.wikipedia.org/wiki/Jack_Cover; https://www.beststungun.com/jack-cover-and-the-taser/
21-22	Julia Child	https://en.wikipedia.org/wiki/Julia_Child
23-24	Bill Couzens	https://www.lesscancer.org/about-us/less-cancer-board-of-directors/william-u-bill-couzens/; https://www.record-eagle.com/sports/local_sports/cycling-through-grief-less-cancer-founder-bill-couzens-turns-pain-into-power/article_9a542182-3c39-11ec-8d86-a7ccd62826db.html
25-26	Mary Granville Delany	https://en.wikipedia.org/wiki/Mary_Delany

Pages	Profile	Resource
27-28	Marcia Duhart	https://www.allbusiness.com/retirement-dealing-with-fiscal-fallout-13998835-1.html; https://www.tributes.com/obituary/show/Marcia-R.-Duhart-89684107
29-30	Steve Finn	https://www.theepochtimes.com/former-cop-who-saw-too-many-kids-lives-end-badly-starts-christian-school-to-give-them-2nd-chance_4009396.html
31-32	Gerry Fiorgilio	https://overfiftyandoutofwork.com/blog/older-entrepreneurs-gerry-fioriglio/; https://family-caregivers.com/about-us/
33-34	Lisa Gable	https://www.inc.com/8over80/2007/1-lisa-gable-the-grandmother-of-invention.html
35-36	Carol Gardner	https://www.dogster.com/lifestyle/zelda-english-bulldog-carol-gardner-interview; https://lumitylife.com/blogs/news/multi-millionaire-carol-gardner-72-on-why-it-s-never-too-late-to-become-an-entrepreneur
37-38	John Glenn	https://en.wikipedia.org/wiki/John_Glenn
39-40	Leo Goodwin	https://en.wikipedia.org/wiki/Leo_Goodwin_Sr.; https://en.wikipedia.org/wiki/GEICO
41-42	Ruth Handler	https://en.wikipedia.org/wiki/Ruth_Handler; https://en.wikipedia.org/wiki/Mattel https://www.washingtonpost.com/archive/local/2002/04/29/barbie-doll-creator-ruth-handler-dies/76bfe4ad-d4aa-431f-9c45-16b9b33046fd/

Pages	Profile	Resource
43	Angie Higa	https://www.hawaiibusiness.com/entrepreneurs-after-age-50/; https://skydreamsllc.com/pages/our-chief-everything-officer
44	Duncan Hines	https://en.wikipedia.org/wiki/Duncan_Hines
45	Edmond Hoyle	https://en.wikipedia.org/wiki/Edmond_Hoyle
46	Arianna Huffington	https://en.wikipedia.org/wiki/Arianna_Huffington
47-48	John & Kathy Huggins	https://www.forwardfrom50.com/blog/john-kathy-huggins-building-a-community-while-living-their-rv-dream/
49	Colin King	https://www.educationquizzes.com/; https://www.theguardian.com/small-business-network/2013/aug/02/starting-a-business-after-retirement
50-51	Ray Kroc	https://en.wikipedia.org/wiki/Ray_Kroc; https://en.wikipedia.org/wiki/McDonald%27s
52-53	Sune Larsson	https://www.theguardian.com/small-business-network/2013/aug/02/starting-a-business-after-retirement
54-55	Olive Lynch	https://www.nj.com/new_jersey_women_in_business/2012/03/woman_entrepreneur_of_the_week_olive_lynch_green_waste_technologies.html; https://thestoryexchange.org/cool-entrepreneurial-women-story-exchange/; https://www.youtube.com/watch?v=MJ4_ElCtlFo

Pages	Profile	Resource
56	Bernie Marcus	https://en.wikipedia.org/wiki/Bernard_Marcus
57	Randall Mitchell	https://www.wfaa.com/video/features/man-finds-his-calling-to-make-quilts-for-foster-kids-graduating-high-school/287-b861039f-a81c-4f0b-9e12-70aa2d9c1963
58	Taikichiro Mori	https://peoplaid.com/2021/05/27/taikichiro-mori/
59-60	Anna Moses	https://en.wikipedia.org/wiki/Grandma_Moses
61-62	Clara Peller	https://en.wikipedia.org/wiki/Clara_Peller
63-64	John Stith Pemberton	https://en.wikipedia.org/wiki/John_Stith_Pemberton; https://en.wikipedia.org/wiki/Coca-Cola
65-66	Deborah Ramsey	https://www.foxbusiness.com/features/why-older-workers-are-creating-their-own-jobs
67	Peter Mark Roget	https://en.wikipedia.org/wiki/Peter_Mark_Roget
68-69	Col. Harland Sanders	https://en.wikipedia.org/wiki/Colonel_Sanders
70-71	Judith Sheindlin	https://en.wikipedia.org/wiki/Judy_Sheindlin
72	Ernestine Shepherd	https://en.wikipedia.org/wiki/Ernestine_Shepherd; https://ernestineshepherd.net/?page_id=2; https://madamenoire.com/1042953/everday-women-over-50-fitness/

Pages	Profile	Resource
73-74	Fouja Singh	https://en.wikipedia.org/wiki/Fauja_Singh; https://religionnews.com/2019/04/22/worlds-oldest-marathoner-at-108-is-a-model-of-more-than-simply-stamina/
75-76	Sam Taylor	https://www.theguardian.com/small-business-network/2013/aug/02/starting-a-business-after-retirement
77-78	Mary Tennyson	https://www.aarp.org/work/careers/getting-rich-after-50/
79-80	Julie Wainwright	https://www.cnbc.com/2017/07/20/a-60-year-old-entrepreneur-took-her-business-from-zero-to-500-million.html; https://en.wikipedia.org/wiki/Julie_Wainwright
81-82	Michelle Weidenbenner	https://www.forwardfrom50.com/blog/michelle-weidenbenner-helping-a-million-moms-close-the-gap-between-havoc-and-hope/
83-84	Thomas West	https://www.williamsnews.com/news/2021/jun/29/business-beat-coffee-sales-help-veterans-and-their/
85	Laura Ingalls Wilder	https://en.wikipedia.org/wiki/Laura_Ingalls_Wilder
86-87	Mary Jane Williams	https://www.forwardfrom50.com/blog/mary-jane-williams-when-you-find-your-why-the-rest-falls-into-place/
88-90	Greg Gerber	Personal story by author

www.ingramcontent.com/pod-product-compliance
Lightning Source LLC
Chambersburg PA
CBHW061210070526
44583CB00025B/3193